Blessed by the Light

Todd Thompson

authorHOUSE®

AuthorHouse™
1663 Liberty Drive
Bloomington, IN 47403
www.authorhouse.com
Phone: 1-800-839-8640

First published by AuthorHouse 02/07/2011

ISBN: 978-1-4567-3275-2 (sc)
ISBN: 978-1-4567-3274-5 (e)

Printed in the United States of America

Contents

Introduction

This book is about God's love. I thank Him for the courage he gave me to write it, after thinking about it for some time now. I hope it can help others to have more faith in Him. Many things happened to us, but God got us through them all. You don't always realize it at the time but when you look back and think about how you made it to where you are, it only happened because God made it happen. There is no other way or explanation.

We are so fortunate to have a Father in heaven who is our father on earth. He will also be our father for eternity, if we accept Jesus, His son, as our personal savior. God has always been there for me. Every situation, problem, moment, good times and the tough times, He has never left my side. I might have moved from Him at times, but through His love, grace, and mercy He has never moved. When I call to Him, He answers-at His time not mine, but He always answers. It is all about trust and it can be very difficult at times, but you can't reason it. Just let go and let God. He will always provide a way, an out, a solution, when you think and believe that there isn't one. His ways are higher than our ways. Life is hard; I don't know how people can live without

God in their lives. I constantly seek God and ask Him for help and wisdom and for Him to give me the skills and or qualities needed at the time I need it. Some people might think that this is a weakness, but I would rather be strong in Him and be successful than going on my own abilities and strength. But you have to ask Him to show you what to do. I doesn't matter what you feel, what matters is what you believe and think.

Trust Him and turn your life over to Him, the one who made you and you will become the person that God created you to be. Why wait? This book is a true account of events that did happen. Some things might be hard to believe. God will intervene whenever He wants to, and when He does He will get results. It is also important to remember that we are in a spiritual battle with good and evil. Choose to be on God's team and you will win!

Chapter 1: Growing Up

One of the earliest memories of growing up was when I was about four years old. I heard screaming and crying upstairs from my mom. I went up there with my older brother and sister, who were about five and six years old at the time. Our dad was trying to drown our mom in the bathtub. I remember it as if it were yesterday. The fear and helplessness was paralyzing. I remember us kids talking about getting help from someone. We were crying and yelling at our dad to stop it. It was like a bad dream. My older brother did go to get help. He ran over to the neighbors and they called the police. Our mom was saved that night by God's grace.

The last memory I have of my dad, which was the last time I saw him, was when I was a junior in high school. We had finally moved out for good to another place. It was an older house, but we didn't care. Man, we were so happy, because he was not around. We didn't care that we lived off of the government cheese (and other government food) and that we had to use food stamps. We loved not having to live in fear. We didn't care that we wore clothes from garage sales. I didn't care as much that his name would still come up on the radio when he would get into trouble with the law, which was embarrassing and humiliating the older I got. It was great: we could have friends over and do normal stuff for once.

However, the last time I had to deal with him physically was this night. It was a very cold night in January in 1982. A friend of mine and I were hanging out and actually doing some homework. My younger brother and sister and mom were home. Suddenly mom yelled out, "He's here," and then *crash*, he broke down the first door with an ax handle. I told my friend to take the two little ones downstairs and hide. I looked out and he was now breaking in the third door, on the porch. I grabbed my mom and a good-sized knife on the counter while we ran around to the other side of the living room. He came walking in, and I had my mom next to my right side, with the knife ready.

I was praying furiously, *God please make it so that he cannot see us. Send your angels.* I knew that I would have to confront him and it would not be pretty. I did not want to kill him, but I was ready to do what I had to do. I thought that I would have to injure him for sure by beating him to the punch. I remember being calm. Mom was trying not to cry and I was ready. He walked around the corner and was about seven or eight feet away from us. It was slightly dark, and he stopped. I turned my head slightly and was looking straight at him. We were against the wall and I could swear he was looking not at us, but *through* us. It was so amazing that he could not see us. This seemed to take forever. I was waiting for him to swing that weapon at us and I was going to use mine on his shoulder area. I just wanted to wait first, while still beating him to the first move.

He walked out of the room and back outside. I waited about a minute or so, then ran out to the kitchen and called the police to come over. It was freezing in the house with the doors off. I looked up; the phone was near the front doors and he was coming back in. I thought, *Oh man*, and then the cops showed up. They were having a standoff with him and my older brother was outside and tackled him. They also found a gun on him.

The more I thought about that night, the more I know that God saved us. The praying my mom and I did worked! If he had seen us it would have been over.

I didn't know he had a gun. I think he had gone back to his car to get it and was coming back to the house. I also thought, *What if I had killed him?* That would not have been easy to live with. But we had survived—again. Of course everyone found out about it in town and it was on the radio the next day. It was hard dealing with the craziness and/or embarrassment of our dad doing stuff like this. I just tried to do the best I could and work hard at not letting it get to me.

You can probably figure out that most of the years growing up before that were not that great either. They weren't, but we did learn that we could rely on God for protection and help. Growing up was very hard, but we were becoming survivors. We relied on each other, our mom and our grandparents as well. As a little kid I used to pray so hard at night when he would come home drunk and start hitting our mom or one of us, and I would keep praying until it stopped, usually after an hour or two, sometimes more. We would worry, cry, and pray. I think back and wonder how we got through all of that. These are some of the times when God protected us. God saved us well over a hundred times growing up. I was in first grade when he burned our house down. Fortunately, we were staying at our grandparents place at the time. From time to time we would leave and stay with them or with friends when things got really bad. But he would never leave for good and law enforcement never did enough. He might be in jail overnight and that was it. As we were growing up, he left and came back many times. He would also take us all out in his car and say he was going to roll it or run into something. He never actually did wreck the car, but I remember the crying and yelling. He would keep threatening that he was going to do it, and I thought that he would. I also remember that law enforcement was afraid of him. There is no way that today a person could get away with so much. One time the deputy sheriff came over to talk to him about something he had done. After arguing for a couple minutes, R. T. (as I will refer to our dad) hit him so hard he was out cold, lying over the stove. The deputy crawled out to his car and left. He never came back either. R. T. was never arrested for that, unbelievable.

It was the same with social services. Everyone knew what was going on, but there was never any help from the Department of Human Services or anyone else. Maybe nothing was ever reported or those services were not available back then. Things were different in the 70s, I guess. As a kid I just remember hoping that someone would step in and help, but it didn't happen that way. It didn't stop at all.

Not long after that we were at our grandparents' place out in the country. We got a call that R. T. was up on a hill with a high-powered rifle and was going to shoot at us. After a long afternoon, a relative found him up there with his rifle and drinking beer. I don't remember any shots being fired, but it created another big, messed-up deal.

When my brother and I were in upper elementary, around fifth and sixth grade, R. T. had new adventures for us. During the day he would check out old abandoned farms to see what they had. He would then wake us up late in the night and say we were going to hunt rabbits. We would go with him to these spooky places out in the middle of nowhere and take stuff out of these houses. We used to be so scared, staying close to each other as much as we could.

We couldn't use flashlights and I remember always grabbing some kind of tool for a weapon and putting it in my back pocket. We also took scrap metal and junk to sell. We would get home and go to bed, but still go to school. One time we were up until morning so that we could go sell the stuff to a guy. A week or two went by and he told us, "Are you guys ready to go rabbit hunting again?" Boy, did I ever dislike this guy. We knew this was wrong, but we had to do what he told us to do. Being scared will certainly make you pray.

In regards to praying, we were Catholic and lived close to the church. I was an altar boy, some weeks attending Mass every day of the week. I always felt safe and peaceful at church. I always thought I could feel the presence of God there the most. We also attended a Catholic elementary and middle school. I did always feel that God was with me, and I prayed to him a lot.

It gave me a sense of peace, and I knew he was present. But why was all this stuff always happening with our dad? Our mom had many meetings with the priest, whom we liked a lot. Every time she said she was going to see him about R. T., I was hopeful. We saw the priest as being close to God, and God would probably do what he asked for. Things pretty much stayed the same, though. We would continue to hope and pray. I knew we really couldn't rely on anyone but God himself. At an early age, I had a relationship with God. I always felt that I could never be hurt with him at my side. This was really my only hope I had, even at a young age. Nobody else could help us.

We moved out to another place to rent for a while. I was now in middle school and started to engage in juvenile delinquent behaviors. I would drink, smoke, and do stupid stuff with some friends we didn't care about anything and just wanted to have fun. I learned these behaviors and was now trying them out. I finally came to my senses; this wasn't right and it wasn't me. I got involved in sports and that helped me to set some goals and to focus on positive things. I quit doing that stupid stuff and concentrated on sports for the most part.

When my brother and I were in junior high, our dad had a new job for us. He would take us to load scrap and junk metal. Over the summers we would take turns, going out with R. T. all day. Was this fun or what? He would pay us a few bucks a day and all the water we wanted, from morning until dark. I usually didn't say anything to him all day, I just did what he told me and made sure I didn't make him mad. I would just throw the junk in and made sure it was stacked right. These were the longest days of my life. We couldn't wait for school to start just to get away from him. On some of the worst nights, he would stop in a bar and I would have to sit there all dirty, waiting for him to finish. I had never disliked anyone like this. By the time we would get home most nights, it was too late to do anything. But I was helping to provide for our family—that was the only good thing about it.

Starting high school proved to be a good thing. Throwing this junk metal around all day got me into pretty good shape. This proved to be helpful in sports, and that's all I thought about, and practicing whenever I could. It was something positive and fun too. But at the same time, R. T. was not changing at all. He seemed to be getting even worse. One night he was hitting my mom and I was there. I wish I had grabbed him or something, but I stood there, and he kept saying, "Come on. I'll put you in the hospital." I kept staring at him. I was a freshman and it still bothers me today. I just kind of froze there. He stopped, did a few things to me, and left. Mom had to go to the hospital that night. I could have done a lot more. It bothers me writing about it. It's hard not to cry thinking about this stuff again.

By God's grace she was all right and things were back to being okay for a while that year.

Our family never talked about anything when he was around. We always had to be quiet. We couldn't have any friends over, and most were too scared to come over anyways. We never talked to anyone about what was going on, knowing they would hear about it anyways. I just went on trying to be as normal a kid as possible and separating myself from this stuff. I started to resent the authorities, who refused to step in and help. I also was not proud of my relatives on his side, who would not intervene. They would all stay out of it and stay away. Nobody had any courage to help, except our grandpa and grandma, and all this was very stressful on them. People sure liked talking about what R.T. was doing, but nobody ever did anything about it.

Some other things happened and we moved out to our grandparents' place in the country. We really liked it there, but it was hard on them. They got us an older place back in town to move into and we were in heaven. I was still mad at myself for not doing enough the year before, when he was hitting mom. One weekend, I was drinking some beer with my friends and planned to go over to where he lived and fight him, one on one, for everything he had done to us. I was pretty pumped up as I walked up to the door. I pounded on the door and it was locked. I was planning on punching him as many times as I could when he opened the door. He never came to the door. I don't think he was there. We left, but I would be ready for the next opportunity.

There was a court hearing that we kids had to go to and testify. R. T. told all kinds of lies and said very hurtful things about some of us. He was put in jail for a while after he got caught stealing crates of gunpowder from some abandoned farm. The news on the radio was embarrassing, but at least we didn't have to live with him. I couldn't separate myself from this guy. The next and last time I saw him was when he broke in. Like I mentioned earlier, I was ready and willing that night to do whatever I had to do. God had a plan for my life. He was waiting for me to commit to him totally. I thought a little here and a little there for God was good enough. It wasn't. You have to surrender your life to God and commit to him totally. I wasn't doing that. I was relying mostly on myself, and I would pray only when I needed Him to help me. I didn't have a true relationship with God. Perhaps I had when I was younger, but now I felt as if I didn't need him as much anymore. R. T. was gone and I was older.

The church I grew up in did not focus on developing a relationship with God and giving your life to Jesus. It was based on what you did, your works, and God was viewed as someone far away. He might hear your prayers or he might not. You could pray to the saints for intervention or go to the priest. I did that, but it wasn't the right way for me. I wanted more and needed more. But I would put that off for the time being.

Chapter 2: Moving On

I devoted my time and energy to playing sports at this point. That's all that mattered to me. My friends and I would lift weights, run, or play basketball. If we were not playing it, we were watching games on TV. It was a good outlet and a great way to learn self-discipline, teamwork, hard work, and sportsmanship. I would even shovel the snow at night at the park to shoot hoops, no matter how cold it was. This was all good and all for the time being. Even though R. T. was out of the picture, I was still dealing with some emotional scar tissue. It was all emotional stuff now. I wasn't relying on God nearly as much anymore, although he was holding on to me. The sports stuff was going well, until I broke a bone in my leg during a football game. I didn't know it was broken even though the pain was excruciating. For about a week, I tried to tape it and play. Then I went to the doctor. I had some problems with that injury for a long time. It healed, but I had constant pain. This brought me back to God again, because all I could do was pray about the pain and practice and play through it. I thought I was cursed or something now.

This went on for a couple of years and several more

surgeries. I could relate to Job in the Bible somewhat. I thought it had to be some kind of test of faith. I would become one of the team captains in several sports and homecoming king. Sports proved to be a good thing as long as I did not rely totally on it for my happiness and success, as it would soon pass, as most things do.

I went on to college and pretty much did everything on my own. I majored in teaching and coaching. I wanted to have a positive impact on kids' lives. I also liked the idea of having summers off. During college I participated in some sports, but it was hard and I didn't play that much. It was still worth it. At this time in my life, I had become much removed from God, from praying and thinking about him and talking to him as I did when I was younger. I was not living as a Christian should and I was not relying on God whatsoever. I was only focused on achieving and only looking out for myself. I could not have been more selfish. I always thought I had a good heart and was a caring person even then, but I really didn't feel obligated to anyone.

I had some anger issues from the past. I would not take guff from anyone. I would put people in their place and it wouldn't even bother me. I would also fight anyone at any time if there was a reason to. I wasn't afraid of anyone. I wouldn't back down from anyone, even if he was twice my size. This isn't a good or healthy way to live. I finally got over this, but it was not of my own doing. I had moved from God, but He didn't move from me, He was still working in my life and He still loved me as much as ever. He had too, that is His nature. Mercy and grace and love is what God is. I didn't realize this at the time, but looking back I certainly do now.

I got into teaching and coaching. I found myself really liking to help students who came to me with their problems or for advice. I would get to know them pretty well and I showed them that I cared. I could always tell what students came from a broken home or dysfunctional family. I could relate to what they would tell me and I had a lot of empathy for them. I became a school counselor and kept coaching too. This was great, because I could help students who were hurting and also solve some of their problems. I found myself dealing with students with major problems—drugs, alcohol, relationships, suicidal thoughts, etc. I thought I heard most of it, as much as a person could hear. I had lived most of that stuff too, and I had a lot of insight into how they were feeling. The counseling I was trained in helped to stabilize some of their problems temporarily. I started to use what would work because these counseling theories were not working. I would tell students about Jesus, what He had did for me and what He would do for them, if they put their trust in Him, and also asked Him. The problems they had were too big and some of these kids were in hopeless situations. I knew that the ones I worked with were the ones God sent to me so that I could tell them about him. It felt 100 percent right. Telling these students about the power of God and how giving your life to Jesus will change their life had amazing results. It gave them hope and a change of heart. This is the only kind of counseling that I know of that works and I had seen it work. I studied all the other theories, and in my opinion, they do not work, but good listening skills and showing that you care does help. I continued as a counselor for about six years. I would focus my time and energy on helping students with problems, partly because nobody helped me and partly because I felt good doing this. The best part would always be telling them to go to God and to ask him. This didn't always happen, but if the opportunity came up, I certainly would tell them. If matters got serious I would call their parents and let them know what was going on and ask them if it was okay if I did some Christian counseling.

More often than not they were fine with it. Even though I was married at this point, I would supervise and play basketball or spend time after school teaching these kids weightlifting techniques. If they were fishing, I would go there and fish with them too. I was certainly popular, the role model I always thought I could be. I spent most of my time with students that most would call disadvantaged or even losers. I saw their potential and I saw myself in most of them. Even though I was doing all this I still didn't feel right. I felt lonely. I could not understand why I felt so lonely. I didn't give my home life much time or attention. This wasn't it. I always had people around me. Something was missing and I couldn't figure it out. This went on for several years and I would put in more and more time working with students. Growing up in the church that I did, focused mostly on religion, not a relationship with Jesus. Deep down and through all that scar tissue, I knew I had to go back to relying on God, like I did as a little kid.

That's what I wasn't doing though. I was around thirty years old now and we tried to have a child but it would not happen. Things could have been better. I was so wrapped up in other people's problems I didn't work on my own at home. That week we found out that we would be having a baby. I found out the day that it needed to be found out the most. I knew God's hand was in this, because nothing could be this coincidental. Again, I messed up but God fixed it. He was getting me back on His track.

We had a baby girl, and this was the greatest time in my life up to this point. I would now spend all my time at home and I would not have traded it for anything in the world. But for some reason I still had this sick, lonely feeling. It was really starting to bother me. Did I miss my brothers and family? I did miss them some, but not to this extent. That night, the week we got our little one home, my wife and I talked about all the things we were going to do and how great things were going to be now.

We talked about a lot of stuff and I talked about my dad and how he messed things up so much. I thought about how much better I could have been in everything if I had a normal dad. That night I decided to forgive him in my heart. I had to move on and let it go. I was a dad now and I didn't need that weighing me down. I had all the insight and understanding to avoid being like him in any way. I saw all the hurt and damage that he had done to others and me. I told this to many kids that were having problems at home with a parent—that they would not grow up to be like their dad, that in fact they would be just the opposite. They had seen too much and experienced too much pain. Like me, they had too much insight and would be just the opposite. They were good kids with a lot of potential. I always left them with that thought, that they had a lot of potential and they were going to do great things.

That one night, forgiving my dad in my heart would change the rest of my life.

Chapter 3: My Real Father

I never thought what happened next could have happened to me. I had read about things like this in the Bible, but words cannot really give it the respect it deserves. I always believed in God and knew he was real, but I didn't know how close he really is to us all the time. I had always thought that I had committed to giving my life to him and that I was saved, that I would be in heaven someday. I had done this mostly with works and following church procedures and protocols. I never viewed God and Jesus as being my best friend and father, as I know now. It's about having a day-to-day, hour-by-hour relationship. That's the way it should be. He doesn't want what you have or what you do—he wants you! He does hear all of your prayers and he does answer them, if it is His will and in His timing.

It was Super Bowl Sunday, January 28, 1996. I was going to go to the early service at church and then go home. I had stuff to do before the game started and that was on my mind. So I went by myself and sat in the back pew, as usual, wanting to put in my time and then head out. I was thinking about the Super Bowl game and how it might turn out. Just another uneventful day so far. Church finally got started and we stood up to sing the hymn. I felt and saw a gold colored light, which had started at the front of the church at the altar and was coming towards me. It took up most of the middle of the church. I could feel it getting stronger as it slowly moved towards me. I knew when it started that it was God. I don't know how I knew it was God, I just knew. The feeling was love. His presence was slowly coming toward me and getting stronger and stronger the closer it got. I felt very unworthy but extremely grateful and willing to receive this love from God. The feeling was so strong as it surrounded me that I had a hard time withstanding it.

I love my family with all my heart and this was a thousand times stronger than that, if not more. I was feeling God's love. I could not take it all in. I could only take in what I thought I could handle. His love is so powerful that I could not receive all of it. If I did, I didn't think that I could physically bear it, because it was so great. Many people don't realize how much God loves them. If they could just feel his love one time, then they would never have any doubts. I felt and could see twenty to thirty angels that I somehow knew. Each one looked somewhat the same, but they were all different. They knew me and I knew them as the best of friends. I have not known twenty to thirty people that died, but I felt them next to me, as if they had always known me and I had always known them, like brothers. They looked physical in nature but they were spiritual beings. They were close to me, and kind of huddled up next to me.

For the first time in my life this felt right. It could not have felt or been more right. I remember thinking, *hey guys, what took you so long. Man, I missed you.* I don't know or understand how I could have known them, but I did know them and I know that I didn't know them from here on earth. I knew they were from heaven. They were here for me and this moment. I really couldn't make out any faces, but I didn't have too—that didn't matter. They were similar in appearance but still very different I knew each one individually and they knew me. I also felt that they had been with me on this journey in life, and that they felt everything I had felt and experienced growing up. I sensed that with them—that this is the life and/or experience that I had wanted or signed up for. That this was part of my testing in life.

This was all very encouraging, like a support group from heaven. I sensed that life is a test and you have to do your best to pass the test. These angels seemed like family and brothers. I loved each one of them deeply, because I knew them, although I didn't know from where. They had bodies like ours, but in the spirit form.

When the gold light stayed around me, God said, as loudly as anything I have ever heard in my life, almost like it was over an intercom, "Todd, I'm your Father. Don't worry about him anymore. I love you." I started crying and I could not stop. For some reason I had grabbed a different jacket from the one I usually wore and the pocket was full of Kleenex. How coincidental. At this point I was trying to gather myself and His love was so strong. I could not accept all of it, but I wanted too. I felt paralyzed in love. His voice was amazing; I thought everyone heard Him, even though he was communicating to me spirit to spirit. This was by far the greatest thing that had ever happened to me, or could ever happen to me. If people could ever understand how much God loves them, it would change their life. He is all love. He is not what some people might think, sitting way up there somewhere waiting to condemn people. It is hard to explain, but God loves us more than we can imagine, and he knows your name too. Even the very hairs of your head are all numbered (Matthew 10:30, New International Version, henceforth NIV).

None of this would have happened if I had not forgiven my dad that night. Forgiveness is very powerful. It had opened up this door and God rewarded me for forgiving R. T. I was being blessed at this time, and I wished I had forgiven him earlier in my life. God had been waiting and patient with me to forgive.

When this was happening, nobody else saw it or heard it. I looked around and nobody was looking in my direction. God's voice sounded physical, as if it were coming over a loudspeaker, but he was communicating with me spirit to spirit. I didn't say anything back. I was grateful and he knew what I was thinking. I don't know how anyone could not ever believe in God and not think he is a God of love and goodness. Now, at this time, His presence was still upon me during the service, but His presence would get stronger when we sang the hymns at praise time. When we came to sing the second song, another event happened. All this time I am aware of the church service and the people next to me while still being in God's presence. What happened next was amazing!

I was now standing in front of Jesus! I was at the place where He died on the cross. He had just died. He was on the cross with his head down. The sky was black with clouds rushing by and wind blowing, as if some natural disaster was about to strike. I was there! This was the place where Jesus was crucified. I could see three ladies crying and kneeling down at the base of the cross. It was rocky ground and there were large boulders at the foot of the cross where they were praying. I thought I could take a couple steps and touch Him; He wasn't up that high, like the pictures we have all seen. He did look similar to the pictures and drawings of Him. He was beaten up pretty bad, and His eyes were closed. His hair and beard were a dark brown and he had a white garb on around his waist. I knew one of the women kneeling was Mary, the mother of Jesus.

God said, "See what I have done for you." It was the saddest thing I had ever seen but also the greatest. Jesus died for our sins so that we could be with him and God in heaven someday. He paid the penalty of sin for us, since we cannot save ourselves. I had two angels standing next to me when this was happening and we were looking at Jesus together. It was as real as it could be. I wasn't focusing on the two angels who were from the group earlier; I was only focusing on Jesus with all my senses.

When the song was over, I was back in the church pew. The church service seemed like it had lasted only five minutes, but in fact it had been over an hour. I left and got into my car, and a song by Elton John came on the radio: "You'll Be Blessed." I really liked this song because it always reminded me of our daughter when I heard it. I drove around for a while, still crying and in still in shock. I went home and I didn't tell anyone for weeks. That lonely feeling was long gone and has never been back to this day. I wanted to tell some people, but I didn't think they would believe me. I also thought that they would say, "Why you?" I don't use drugs or drink or take medication. I wasn't overly tired or wishing that this would happen in my mind. It happened unexpectedly. I didn't feel worthy of it happening, and I thought about what I would do now. But now I felt gratitude to God and this was between us, and I still think about it daily. I would eventually tell others. God wanted me too. I would tell anyone that God brought to me to share this testimony. I also shared this with some churches and men's groups.

I was going to acknowledge God even though some people wouldn't believe this could happen. Still, I know it did happen, and I would not be ashamed to let others know. If it helped them, then that's all that mattered. Mathew 32 says, "Whoever acknowledges me before men, I will also acknowledge him before my father in heaven" (NIV). Everyone will find out eventually when they die, that everything in the bible is true, but why wait until then? Why not now, especially if it means your eternal salvation. John 3:16 says, "For God so loved the world that he gave his one and only Son, that whoever believes in him shall not perish but have eternal life" (NIV).

Chapter 4: Miracles

God is still in the miracle business. The bible tells about thousands of miracles that happened, and they happened a lot. We cannot see most miracles as they happen, or they happen naturally. Things just seem to work out, or a person thinks he got lucky. I don't think anything is coincidental, and I have a good idea where luck comes from, but sometimes unexplained miracles can and do happen. I had started a new job as a school principal. I thought it was God's calling, even though this might not be the path others would choose.

After a meeting at the school about the expectations for me at this place, I thought I had made a mistake going there. This school had major issues that I didn't find out about at the interview. So I went home late that night. I walked home and said this prayer: "Jesus, I'm really going to need you to get me through this first year at this job. I said this as an example. I'm going to need to grab on to your shirt and just pull me through it. Give me some kind of a sign."

I got home and went upstairs by myself. My wife and daughter were sleeping downstairs. I laid there for a while thinking about this and that. I kept hearing some kind of noise, like something brushing up against something. I didn't even turn around for a while. I thought a window was open and something outside was making the noise. I finally did turn around. What I saw was the door opening and closing by itself. I got up and checked the windows, but they were closed. It wouldn't have mattered, because they had put new carpet in the room and it was hard to open and close the door. I went over to the door and just watched it. It started opening and closing faster. I had never seen anything like this before. It was very weird. I wasn't scared and I didn't feel as if I had to leave. I finally grabbed the door and it stopped immediately. When I grabbed the door, I had also grabbed part of the shirt that was hanging from it. It was flopping up and down pretty fast. I went back to bed and tried to figure what in the world that was all about. I looked over at the door now and then, but it didn't do anything anymore. I didn't realize until the next morning that the prayer I said that night was answered! I now knew it was a sign, and I grabbed the shirttail. I was amazed but more grateful than anything else. I had never asked for a direct sign like that before. Wow, God answers prayers. That incident gave me the confidence to move forward.

Soon after, some other things happened. We decided to take our daughter for a stroller ride that night. We came back and we were sitting outside on the steps. I kept hearing some song playing, no words, just the melody. I thought it was a toy from inside or something. We went in and in the middle of the floor was an old Christmas card, which one of my sisters had sent to me a few years back. It was the kind that sings when you open it. We couldn't figure out how it got there. It wasn't there when we left to go for the walk; we had packed all that stuff away in a box in the closet. I read it, and it was about us getting together for Christmas at home, and how much fun we would have. We didn't make it back that year, so I thought this had to be some kind of sign. I was going to make sure we would make it back for Christmas this year.

We found out that our second child was due Christmas Day, so we decided to have her delivered at the hospital in our hometown and also get together with my mom and sister for Christmas. I knew we had to do this.

Several weeks later my job situation became very challenging. I got home very late that night from another meeting and just went to the couch to try to get some sleep. I prayed, "God, please give me some peace and let me go to sleep." Then, just like that, I felt peaceful. I woke up three or four hours later and saw this light shining on my chest. I looked up and it wasn't coming from anywhere. I looked toward the windows and the blinds were closed. I just stared at the light and could not figure out the source. The room was pitch dark, so I could have figured out pretty quickly if someone was shining it on me.

My wife and daughter were upstairs sleeping. I got up and it was gone. I realized that it was from God. It had made me feel very peaceful and I fell asleep right after I said that prayer. Again I was amazed and grateful. I had never experienced something like this either, but ever since God visited me at church, stuff like this was happening.

It was getting close to Christmas and we were excited about going back to have our baby and to also see my family. We went to my mom's house and my sister and her husband were there. We were talking, and I felt I needed to tell them about what had happened to me at church, and about the door and the light. I do not think they believed me, but I had no reason not to tell the truth. I thought it might help them with their faith. They were my family; why wouldn't I share such experiences? I got to the part involving the light, and as I told them, the most amazing thing happened. I was probably just as shocked as they were. That light was now on the wall, just as I had described it. It was the same light that was on my chest that night, several months earlier it was moving around and then came to rest on my chest again. At first my brother-in-law, who was sitting right next to me on the couch, thought I was doing it. I said, "No way," and showed him my hands. We looked at the window, but my mom's windows blinds were closed. They were in disbelief and wondering what had just happened.

I know they were having a hard time believing me, but then God made that light show up and they saw it. I felt great, not only because they believed me but because God was there and made that happen. I couldn't have made any of this up even if I wanted to. We thought we had seen a miracle and we still talk about that night from time to time. It all went back to that Christmas card. God wanted to perform a miracle for us. It was unbelievably cool. I was glad there were witnesses, but I was happier for them that they could see a miracle like this. Our second child was born the next day. That in itself is just as much of a miracle to me as a light coming from heaven.

I thanked God for these gifts of his love. I couldn't thank him enough. I didn't feel worthy or special or anything like that. It happened only because I had forgiven my dad, and I was seeking God. He knew what I needed. God will make you wait, but he is never late.

The following are some additional events that I thought would be worth mentioning to show that God is right here next to us, waiting for us to call to Him so He can show us He hears us, and will help us.

At one school that I was at, I came up with a reading project to try to motivate elementary students to read some books. I told them that for every book that they read, I would pull a school bus, with a rope, one yard for one book. It was a small school so the number wasn't going to be too high. I gave them a couple weeks to do this. In the meantime I had been experimenting by pulling the bus. It would work pretty good since the road I would start on was slighted slanted down for one block. I practiced pulling it and it was really easy, almost anyone with decent strength could have done it. Once it got rolling it would roll on its own some. The only part that was kind of hard was just getting it moving, which only took a few seconds. So I practiced it several times and I thought I would have to make it look harder than it was more than anything. I wasn't too worried about it. I pulled it at least a block and sometimes a block and a half just in case I had to go farther. The second block actually inclined up a little but it was still pretty easy with the momentum gathered. You could not tell that either street had an incline or decline; they both looked flat, because it wasn't that much. I also was training a lot by doing some heavy weightlifting on the side. I was in pretty decent shape. I wasn't worried at all.

The students did a great job reading their books and the distance total would be 200 yards. About what I expected so that was o.k. The big day arrived and it was really cold that morning, around 20 degrees or so. I made sure I warmed up and stretched out good and all of that. So the teachers lined the streets up with the kids and some other people came up to watch. I got the driver and we went over to get the bus. The one I had practiced with was gone, in fact all the buses we used were out. There was one spare left and it had been sitting there for many days and had not been used. The driver brought it over to the starting line and I just didn't feel good about the situation now. I said some things to the crowd about how the students were making me pull the bus and how much fun they should have watching. They were all excited- which was good.

The driver put the bus in neutral and I put the two ends of the rope over my shoulders and got down low to get it moving. I couldn't believe what was happening, this bus would not even budge, I thought the driver had the brake on or something. This bus sat so long it was like the wheels were froze up or something. I thought man, this cannot be happening. I finally got the thing moving, barely. I had used up a lot of energy just doing this. I knew immediately that I was in trouble. The bus was barely moving and it was certainly not moving freely on its own any at all. I was trying to get some momentum to make it to the half-way point so I could use that momentum for the second half, which was on the incline. I was starting to fade and I was pretty much spent at the half-way point in the middle of the intersection. In fact I thought I had used up most of my energy and I had to stop and kneel down at that half-way point, the last thing in the world that I wanted to do, or that I thought I would have to do.

I heard people sounding disappointing, and saying well you got half-way or good try Mr. Thompson. I wasn't happy at all. Some people were starting to leave. I was kneeling down and praying for God to give me the strength to finish this thing. I was really focused on Phillipians 4:13, "I can do all things in Christ who gives me strength". (N.I.V.)

For some reason the thought came to my mind to switch the ropes to the side of my arms instead of over my shoulders. I just had in my mind that for some reason now I could make it. I probably prayed for about 30 seconds when I had stopped and knelt down. I started pulling it again and it was starting to move a little. I was more determined than ever and I kept focusing on Phill 4:13 with every step I was saying that verse. I could see the cones I put at the finish line at the end of the block and man did they ever look far away. It was one step at a time and it was the hardest physical thing I had ever done or attempted to do. I was in more physical pain than I thought was possible, but the bus was still barely moving and I knew I didn't want it to stop, I needed all of that little momentum to make it. My legs were in so much pain and I was breathing really hard. The kids motivated me because they were cheering. One other thing motivated me was that this school wasn't a good place, the teachers wanted to see me fail and I was going to prove them wrong. I remember the teachers didn't even come out to watch except a couple of them. I was getting closer, but I thought I had done some damage, I was in so much pain I could not hardly feel anything anymore. I had this bottle of Lourdes water my mom had given me earlier that week. She said that people that visited that place in the holy land were healed and had miraculous things happen to them. I could feel it in my back pocket and had earlier forgotten that I had it on me. I was thinking about that now. It was about the last four or five steps from the finish that I knew I would now make it. I did! I was extremely thankful to the Lord in my heart. I could not have done that without Him, there is no doubt in my mind. I remember I fell down and couldn't get up, I tried several times, and my legs were shot. I also thought I might have a heart attack or something because I was still breathing so fast even after several minutes, I couldn't catch my breath. I remember looking up and the kids were all happy. That's all that mattered to me. I looked up and one of the teachers was laughing that I was on the ground, and thought it was funny, for some reason. That summed up the attitude those teachers had there, except one or two, and that is exactly why I would do projects like this for the students there. There was a couple of them there not only laughing but would not even help me get up, they just stood there. It didn't matter, I made it! I got up and the Lord's will prevailed!

At one school where I worked at I dealt with some individuals who were into the occult and witchcraft. Whenever you are doing God's work, the enemy will use and try to send people against you. But God is greater than any problem you will ever have, He is the one in control. So these parents were into using drugs and into some kind of witchcraft, from what I had heard. They had a kid in school that was having all kinds of problems, big surprise. These parents didn't think we were meeting his needs and helping him to be successful. According to them it was my fault and they would call school board members and the superintendent and complain to them about me. We were trying to help their son the best we could and we were doing everything we possibly could. It was their goal to constantly call and complain or come up to the school to complain. I needed some help. I kept praying about the situation and God was going to intervene. The student's dad would call and start swearing whenever I talked to him. The mom would do anything possible to try to ruin my character. They were angry at me because their son had attendance problems and I was going to turn them over to the county attorney. Anyways we had a big meeting planned in my office with them and other school personnel, etc. I had heard how they were going to try to tear me apart and all this and that.

I had about eight or nine chairs in the office that night before the meeting I prayed to God to show me what to do. I blessed the room with some holy Lourdes water that I had and prayed over the room. I put some drops of the water on each chair. I also had a small gold cross that I hung up on the wall right behind my desk and chair. I did this because of my faith, I had prayed about it, and I knew these parents were into the dark side with what they practiced.

So it is the morning of the meeting and everyone comes in to my office to sit down. I was at my desk. The guy who was the Dad immediately focused in on the cross because he was just off to my side. When he looked at me, I would move over some and the cross was right there full in his view. The student's mom sat right in front of me. Everyone else came in and sat down. She started out with these accusations and it was only a couple seconds and she yelled something about the chair being hot! I knew God had something planned but that surprised me as well. I thought it was great. She said something about what's on that chair and everyone just kind of looked at her because it was just a folding metal chair. So she went and sat on another chair with a cushion on it and she yelled the same thing, I can't sit down in here, she said. So when she is talking she is walking back and forth acting real uncomfortable. Nothing she said made any sense. As for the guy he just sat there and stared at the cross and never said anything. God was there and His presence was there and they could not handle it. If that wasn't enough evidence, after that meeting I never heard from them again, they ended up moving somewhere else. Praise the Lord!

At this same school there was another student that moved in and his mom was supposedly involved with the occult. He wasn't with her anymore but he was in foster care now. The foster parents and the student told me some things about his background and it was a sad deal. The kid was loaded with problems and it would be a new start for him here. His parents started to tell me about some of his emotional problems when he was at home. I was calling them a lot or they would have to come up to the school because he was getting into trouble or he would just walk out of school and go home. The parents were trying their best and they were Christians. They said they would play Christian music at home and he would start running around or saying he had a headache and crying when he heard it. They knew something wasn't right. One morning we were gathered around the flag pole for the National Day of Prayer and he came over and heard us praying. He started yelling something and was running around the school in circles. We finally caught him and took care of that, but it was very weird. The other students were scared of him.

It was several days later that he came into my office. We started talking about God and he started to change. The more I talked about God with him the more he started to change. I remembering feeling that something wasn't right here and this kid wasn't right. I asked him about running around that day when he heard us praying and he said it was an act, that he was just trying to get attention and that it had nothing to do with the praying. I never have seen the following before happen like I did here. His voice changed almost completely from a 18 year old kid to a man's voice which was a lot deeper. His facial appearance changed in that he looked different. I don't know how in the world anyone could do this on their own. It was like something from a t.v. show. You could still tell it was him but he wasn't right. I told him I had to make a quick phone call and I called my pastor friend to come over and pick up something he forgot; I didn't say his name over the phone. I knew this kid had something going on here and it wasn't good, in fact it was evil. It got worse. I was talking to him about God and he was saying things about God how he was fake and he wears a costume and things like that. He would start laughing when I said some scriptures to him. I remember that I was glad I had my bible there. If it could not of gotten any stranger, he said something about me that there is no way he could of known. That kind of threw me off a little. I really started to believe that there was another force here. I had a picture of Jesus on my desk; it was a card from someone that I kept because I liked the picture of Jesus on it. When I started talking to him about giving his life to Jesus for protection he jumped over my desk and grabbed the card and was trying to tear it up. When this happened I grabbed him and my pastor friend happened to walk in and grabbed him from behind and ended up on top of the kid on the floor. I called his parents and they came over. The kid was yelling bad stuff about God. We all prayed for him for at least an hour. The pastor was demanding for the boy to come back and whatever spirit this was, to leave. It seemed to take a long time. He finally snapped out of it. It was pretty intense and stressful because it was happening in my office at school as well. They took him home and my friend and I thought it was the real deal. I told him about what happened before he got there and it only verified that there was something evil here. The parents also thought this was happening because it was a spiritual matter and what he was involved with in the past with his mom. It helped that we all thought the same things and we all were giving this to God to handle. God made that unwanted presence leave that boy and the four of us saw it happen. The rest of the year that kid still had problems but nothing like that happened with him again.

God also will talk to you in subtle ways such as a whisper or the Holy Spirit will give you a thought. God also communicates with you from His spirit to yours and through His word, the bible. At one point I had started to write down bible verses that I liked and certain one's that I could read and they would help and/or inspire me. I typed them on a sheet of paper and would put these where I could see them daily. One sheet was on my desk at all times, that I put on a standing clipboard where they were constantly in front of me. I also hung one up at my house. I liked this strategy and it was something very helpful. After a while the sheets either got knocked off or fell off, and I quit looking for them. At night I started waking up every morning at 4:20 for some reason. It didn't matter what time I went to bed, it would always be the exact same time.

I started to ask God and prayed why this was so? I thought there had to be some kind of reason for it because it was too coincidental. I got out my bible one morning and I didn't know where to start, I did think it had to do with a verse 4:20. God guided me to go to the book of Proverbs and I did. I went to Proverbs 4:20, and this is what it said, "My son, pay attention to what I say: listen closely to my words. Do not let them out of your sight; keep them within your heart. I knew right then and there that is what God was getting my attention for. He was right, I had to get those verses back up in front of me at all times, and I did. The more I would keep His words where I could see and read them, the better off I was. This might have not been a big deal to a lot of people, but it was to me. This was also now one of my favorite verses and a reminder that God is always, always on top of things.

Another quiet incident involving God's whisper was when I went for a long bike ride one night. It was on a bike trail out in the country before it was starting to get dark on a Saturday night. I was thinking about some meetings coming up at school and kind of worrying about how they would go. I wasn't thinking very positive. I had my I-pod on listening to some Christian music and was thinking about God providing a way. I remember specifically thinking that God will make a path, if I trust in Him. I stopped before riding in on the trail to do something with the IPod and this older guy was walking out. It was starting to get kind of dark and it was out in the middle of nowhere. There wasn't any car around or any people. He said there's a tree down about four miles. I said o.k. thanks and that was about it. I didn't think too much of that. Certainly enough there was a good size tree down across the trail about four or five miles in. I didn't think that I could move it otherwise I would of. I like to lift heavy things, just to see if I can I guess. I looked it over pretty good and thought I didn't have a chance. I just got off my bike and walked it around it. The only hassle was that there was a hill I had to go down and around and back up the trail. I kept riding to the end of the trail. It was getting darker now and I started to head back the same way I came in. There was nobody around and I didn't see anyone or hear anyone except that older guy that was walking out when I was coming in earlier I was getting closer to that tree; it was probably a half hour later now when I had first come upon the tree. When I got closer I could see the tree was moved just enough for me to stay on the trail and ride by it, about a yard. I rode over the exact spot that I could not have ridden before, on the same side of the trail. I talked to God in my mind and said, did you have an angel move that tree? He said no, I did. God provides a path, he didn't have to give me this sign but He did! I was thinking about Him providing a path for me before I even entered the trail. Amazing!

Chapter 5: Bringing God Back into the Public Schools

Someone once said as long as there are tests in school, there will be prayer in school. That is true, but we need much more than that. There are so many problems in the public school system because God has been removed. The Ten Commandments were taken out around 1980. Prayer was taken out before then. Some schools do not even say the Pledge of Allegiance anymore, because of the phrase "one nation under God." One can see the escalation of serious problems since then. School shootings were unheard of back then, but now we hear about them more than we want to. I have been to meetings with some of the best experts in the country about how to have a safe school, and they don't have any answers to why these things are happening. Many of us know why they are happening. We need God and prayer back in school.

If somebody has a better answer, I would like to know what it is. Our young people comprise 100 percent of our future. It was now my mission and purpose to acknowledge God in a public school. I could no longer work at one and have a clear conscience if I did not view this as Christian service. All that I would do was, and still is, legal. Most people that work in public schools are good people; they do a good job teaching responsibility, citizenship, sportsmanship, and character development. However, we don't do a very good job acknowledging God in our public school systems. There are some exceptions out there, though. A lot of people think that the separation of church and state means that you cannot mention God's name in school, or not participate in any type of Christian activities. This could not be farther from the truth. You can still have this separation and have God in the school. There are equal-access laws and First Amendment rights for groups and teachers. There are Christian law organizations that will support and verify what you can do legally, and this is far more than what people tend to think. But it seems anti-Christian groups will interpret the same law differently than Christian organizations.

This fear of doing something illegal has made people and schools avoid doing even what is perfectly legal. People use fear like a baseball bat in an attempt to keep Christian programs out of public schools. People think they might lose their job or get in trouble by showing Christian values, while this couldn't be farther from the truth. It comes down to this question: Are people willing to check their Christianity at the door when they walk in every day? I certainly was not going to do this. If some people had questions on the effectiveness of acknowledging God, I would tell them to just try it and see if it works, nobody ever came back and said it wasn't working.

One of the first things I did as a middle school and high school principal was to have the Pledge of Allegiance said every day. By saying "one nation under God," we acknowledge God. I believe that God has blessed the schools that do this. I also believe that acknowledging him will be the best security system we could have. We never had any problems with security in our school. We also started Christian athlete/student clubs. This would be a chance for students to get together for Christian activities, such as Bible studies, prayer time, ping-pong/basketball tournaments, support groups, service projects, and more. They would meet during the day, just as the other school clubs would. The groups were student led and the teacher would facilitate the meetings.

We would bring in the best motivational and character-development speakers I could find in the country, and they were Christians. They would tell their stories, including why they were the way they were, and explaining that it was because of their faith. They exposed their values but did not impose them, or have an altar call. Nobody was ever offended and the meetings went extremely well. The messages were always about doing your best—making good decisions, doing the right thing, citizenship, caring for others, etc. The Bible covers all these principles.

Another program we initiated was called Release Time Education. By federal law, states set aside a certain amount of time every week for students to study religion off campus. Our state allows one hour a week to do this. We set up for a local church/building to provide this time for our students. We would transport them if it was not within walking distance. This can be a great program for students to learn about the Bible, to improve their relationship with Jesus, and to praise and worship. This was approved by the school boards provided that parent permission was obtained. Many times the student leaders would lead the meetings as well. Parents were invited to attend but the teachers could not be a part of it. This not only helped students to grow as young Christians, but some even gave their lives to Christ, and the change we saw in the students was amazing. These are the things that people working at a school would notice. What happened? It is all positive and these students were doing better in school.

Several times during the year we have opportunities for the school and community to get together and pray for our leaders, our country, the community, and our schools. The one day in the spring is called "The National Day of Prayer" and the one in the fall is called "See You at the Pole." We would open this up to everybody and gather around our flagpole before school would start. The students would pray as well, if they wanted to. Everyone would be given a chance to say a prayer or say whatever they wanted too. What a great way to publicly acknowledge our Lord and also to demonstrate that being a Christian is something to be proud of. We would have some school employees show up as well. One summer we opened the school for about three hundred students to stay for a week and they painted houses in the area for needy families. There were Christian speakers and Christian bands at night. It was a Christian-based mission project for students in the surrounding states to attend. It was great, and they left a message of hope and love with the families that the students and leaders worked for. It had a positive impact on everyone involved with it.

One-on-one talks and meetings can be the most effective way to help someone. Often students would come in with problems or helpless situations. I have had students give their life to Jesus right there in the office. You can answer any question a student asks you. If they would ask me anything associated with God, I would give them an honest answer. This is how God works. At night or the morning before school would start I would say, "Dear God, send anyone to me who you want me to witness to about you." Try it—it works.

God would provide opportunities for me to tell others about him. This might happen at a senior breakfast, at graduation, or during a meeting with parents and students. I would always do my best to acknowledge God, because of my love for him and what he has done for me. I could not do it any other way. How could I? I have never put pressure on anyone or required anyone to do anything. It's about opening doors for others and putting the ball in their court to listen and to make a decision, or not. God gives us all the free will to accept or reject him.

There was once a tragedy in the community involving a student's family. The Student Christian Group wanted to do something for the kids involved and for other friends of theirs who were also hurting. The student body was called down to the gym, and if somebody didn't want to participate they didn't have to. We made a huge circle and went around; students could say something or pass. We had almost 100 percent participation with the students and teachers. Most students mentioned God and how we needed him to help us and the family. It was truly amazing! This wasn't something planned; it came together in about fifteen minutes, because people's hearts were in the right place. The students in the student Christian club would put up Bible verses on their lockers throughout the hallway. This was also amazing. Nobody ever messed with them or tore them down. The students sent a message out, and it was all positive.

One of the main reasons why these programs were successful is that we would set up a prayer group to meet regularly and to pray. It was obvious that the prayers were working. We would always see evidence—sometimes immediately, sometimes later on. It would always be according to God's timing. He was working things out and sometimes we just needed to have more faith and to be patient in him. Sometimes he would make us wait, but he was never late.

God can see the situation past, present, and future, just like looking at a yardstick. We can't see it, because if we did, we wouldn't need any faith. We have to trust in God. If our will was his will, then things would happen quickly. Be a bridge builder for God it will mean everything to the person you help. Even if it is only one, it is 100% to that person.

The Bridge Builder, by Will Allen Dromgoole

An old man, going a lone highway, came at the evening, cold and gray, to a chasm, vast and deep and wide, through which was flowing a sullen tide. The old man crossed in the twilight dim: the sullen stream had no fears of him: be he turned, when safe on the other side, and built a bridge to span the tide. "Old man," said a fellow pilgrim, near, "you are wasting strength with building here; your journey will end with the ending day; you never again must pass this way; you have crossed the chasm, deep and wide—why build you a bridge at the eventide?" The builder lifted his old gray head: "Good friend, in the path I have come," he said, "there followeth after me today, a youth, whose feet must pass this way. This chasm that has been naught to me, to that fair-haired youth may a pitfall be. He, too, must cross in the twilight dim: good friend, I am building the bridge for him."

Chapter 6: The Enemy

When you are doing God's work, you will be involved in spiritual warfare. What I mean by this is that God is real, and so is Satan. Satan's mission is to slow down and/or stop anything that will give God glory and honor. Satan will attack you and your family through your weaknesses, and if he can't mess with your mind he will try to attack your health. At one point I would have severe stomach pains—they just happened. The doctors couldn't figure them out and there wasn't any medicine that would work. I just dealt with it for about two years, and one day it was gone. Daily constant prayer broke the strong-hold of it.

A person cannot take the enemy on by himself and expect to win. You can take him on by having the Holy Spirit in you, through Jesus. Ephesians 6:10 says, "Put on the full armor of God" (NIV) and the Bible says, "Greater is He who is in you-referring to Jesus, than he who is in the world-referring to the devil". I believe that God had me grow up with the kind of dad I had to help prepare me to take on this enemy. I learned a lot growing up about how to fight by having God fight for you ("The battle is the Lord's"). David, from the bible, said, "the battle is the Lord's", out loud as he was slinging the stone at Goliath. The battle is the Lord's and we need to do our part and move forward, as God calls us to do. I found the devil's schemes, deceptions, and attacks very obvious and related to doing God's work. Whenever we had a victory, such as a successful prayer rally at the flag pole, or me saying some inspirational facts about God at a breakfast or a graduation, something very challenging would happen soon after, usually some kind of attack on my character or some false accusation or criticism. It would usually happen soon after the event, and it would come from out of nowhere. If I had ever charted this data, it would be so obvious to nonbelievers that this was happening. Those of you who have engaged in this know what I am talking about. Satan will use people, nonbelievers and Christians who claim to be Christians but are not really living as one should.

A Christian out of fellowship with God is one that doesn't regularly confess their sins and are not attempting to live for him daily. Many people go to church and go through the motions, but that doesn't mean they are in line with God, and they might not even be saved. You have to accept Jesus Christ as your personal savior in order to be saved. Mark 16:16 says, "Whoever believes and is baptized will be saved, but whoever does not believe will be condemned" (NIV).

I had some battles trying to start up some of the Christian programs I talked about. The battle would always escalate when more kids would get involved or if the program would grow. Suddenly there would be complaints about things that were not happening. Again, other school clubs would have the same number of students, if not less, have just as many meetings and would not be under attack or criticized like the student Christian Athlete Club was. I tell you it is a spiritual matter. The devil thinks he has won the public school system and that it cannot be a place of Christian values. Many kids have not been reached by the churches, and for whatever reason they do not grow up as young Christians. This is why the enemy attacks are so strong and frequent—he thinks a public school is his territory. This is true for most schools, because they have let this happen. All it takes is one person to change things. But remember, God can and will defeat the enemy for you. As it says in 2 Thessalonians 3:3, "But the Lord is faithful, and he will strengthen and protect you from the evil one."(N.I.V.)

Sometimes it might not seem that way, and we have to go through this stuff. If God was the number-one ranked team in the country, which he is, and the devil is second, it would not even be close—the game would be a blowout. God kicked him out of heaven and gave him some authority on Earth because of man's sin, and God will defeat him for good when the end times come. It's good to remind yourself of this: the battle has already been won, when Jesus went to the cross. We have won—see the last page of the Bible! We still need to be his hands and feet as part of showing our love for him.

I had many battles trying to get several Christian clubs up and running for students. I have had people above me and below me try to get me fired, set me up, or use unethical tactics because they did not like what I stood for. Again, you have to defend yourself, but leave all the consequences to God. I learned that you cannot take all matters into your hands and be revengeful, but you must forgive and move on.

Pray for your enemies, even though it is hard to do that sometimes. Leave all the consequences to God, as Romans 12:19 says: "Do not take revenge, my friends, but leave room for God's wrath, for it is written: 'It is mine to avenge: I will repay, says the Lord'" (NIV). Sometimes you just have to get out of God's way. He keeps the books. I say this prayer a lot, and it will work for you too: "God, I believe you will defeat the enemy and cause him to flee from me as I resist him and put my trust in you." I have had many conversations with students during critical stages in their lives involving serious problems, as I mentioned. Usually, if not always, I would be interrupted or distracted every time I mentioned God's name. Somebody would start pounding on the door and not stop, or the phone would keep ringing, even though I had received no constant interuptions as if they were emergency situations earlier that day. Coincidence?

One time I was counseling a student whom God had brought to me. I told him that only God can help him with the problems he was having. His problems and situation were too great for anyone to solve, but not too big for God. Several times, at the exact moment before I mentioned Jesus's name, the fire alarm would go off and nobody pulled it. This happened three times with the same student, going over the same problem on different days I met with him. It also would happen during Christian Club meetings and prayer gatherings around the pole, but it wouldn't last long.

A very good friend of mine came to our school every year in the fall and spring to motivate the kids to do their best, and he had a Christian message while accomplishing this. He is the best in the country at helping kids to reach their potential. He would make references to God and to Jesus as part of his story, near the end of his presentation. Kids need to hear this, because this is what will help them to be their best.

I would also help to get him into other area schools to give his presentation. This was great, because his message was all about hope and doing what's right. All schools try to develop students character, and this is a great way to do just that. He always got standing ovations and was accepted in the best way possible. Many kids would want to talk to him afterwards and write him letters. We had to pray over his assemblies because the enemy would try to hinder our efforts. Suddenly the microphone would fail to work when he was there; sometimes the equipment wouldn't work. It wouldn't last, but there would always be some kind of distraction that we had to take care of or work around. The enemy's attacks would get stronger the closer we got to our assemblies. My friends involved with these assemblies would call me to see how things were progressing. We would pray for each other because we knew this would help, we had each other's back. I remember the first night I was going to have him do an assembly at one of the schools I was at. That night I kept getting woken up, and I knew something was wrong. I would go back to sleep and then I heard different sounds coming from the girls' room around 2 a.m. I had an uncomfortable feeling that something wasn't good. I had bad vibes about it and was kind of puzzled. It wasn't like the door incident at all, where I sensed a good feeling about it. I went in there and there were five or six toys going off/playing at the same time, they were battery operated. The girls were sleeping. I said in the name of Jesus of Nazareth get out of here, and it all stopped. I know this sounds kind of out there, but it is the absolute truth.

Our schools are a mission field. We had this Christian speaker back at that school every year for five years, and he also visited around thirty-five other schools in the area. The enemy was trying to intimidate me that night because of the impact this man had when he visited schools. The enemy, Satan, doesn't just want to make you look bad and hurt you; he wants to destroy you. As it says in 1 Peter 5:8, "Be self-controlled and alert. Your enemy the devil prowls around like a roaring lion looking for someone to devour" (NIV). That's why it is serious business and you have to be right with God, have your armor on, and rely on God to defeat the enemy for you, while you stand firm and do what God wants you to do. Ephesians 6:10–11: says, "Finally, be strong in the Lord and in his mighty power. Put on the full armor of God so that you can take your stand against the devil's schemes" (NIV)

People who do not engage in doing God's work and are not serious about their relationship with Jesus are not always under attack. If they do not pose a threat they are usually left alone. They will have to answer to God and give an account, though. Psalm 55:22 says, "A righteous man may have many troubles but the Lord delivers him from them all" (NIV).

It might seem that a person who is trying to seek God and do his will is loaded with problems. That is probably true. God wants to test you not only so you can have a "test-imony" but also so that others can observe how you handle certain situations. Your life might be the only Bible some people read. No matter what I have done or have been through, it has all been worth it, because God has been involved. I have no regrets and would do it again, but that would be very tough.

God has to break a person sometimes before he can use him. I'm sure that has happened to me. God gives us adversity in life so that we can rely on him. It's not always what we get, but it's what we have in him that matters. One more thing to remember, God doesn't always call the qualified, but He will qualify the called. He will equip you to do what he wants you to do, so there really is no need to worry.

Chapter 7 School Number One

I wrote a poem called, "The Coach", because it summed up a situation that I was dealing with at the time at one particular school. God opened a door and brought me to this school. It was a place which badly needed Christian educators because this public school was not neutral towards religion, like they are supposed to be. They were hostile towards it. This came from the administration and the enemy uses certain people in power when that person allows it. It is amazing how much good or bad one person can do that has the authority to do so. Anyways God doesn't always send His physicians to people or places that are well. There was a spiritual battle going on at this place. There were different groups with different beliefs because of their backgrounds and the past traditions and history there. I did do a lot of evangelizing and Christian counseling in my office. As mentioned earlier with victories spreading the gospel in a public school setting, which was all legal. It is all about how you do it. But spiritual forces are real and I will talk about how the enemy used the people in charge of this school. This school actually did have a strong Christian student club called the "The Christian Student Athletes" for a short period of time. Due to the leadership from one person. The Christian Student Athletes group was made up of any students that wanted to be part of it. You didn't have to be an athlete, because anyone could join, and everyone is out for physical education or might work out on their own or just like to bike or run, etc. The club is student led with a coach or sponsor acting as a facilitator. The club can meet during the school day like other school clubs do. The can do Christian based readings, activities, bible readings/study, sharing testimony's, attend sporting events, play in school tournaments such as ping pong, basketball, volleyball, etc. The bible is their playbook and they can use it to discuss daily life situations. The administration there did not approve of the group, but it was legal and they could not stop them from meeting. The group had a lot of students involved and parent support. Their leader left and the group was taken over by another person for a year. The club membership dropped in numbers and they did not have as many activities or meetings. I was helping out as an assistant and started to take over the small group bible study class after school. There were only three or four students involved at this time, but we did what we could do. That year the coach in charge of it resigned at the end of the school year. They had some controversial school board meetings about cancelling the program, and it was in the local paper. It was the following year and nobody wanted to be the sponsor for the group, in fact nobody wanted to touch it. I felt obligated to be the sponsor. In my heart God told me to go do it. It was several weeks into school and I put a note into the daily announcements that if anyone was interested in joining the Christian Athletes club to meet after school in the lunch room. These announcements were used daily to advertise all school functions and events. After that was read the fireworks began and it did not end until the end of that school year.

The building administrator had me go into his office and was telling me about how I was breaking the law and how illegal the announcement was because I had the announcement read in school using the school intercom. Even though I was planning on meeting them after school, it was supposedly illegal because of the separation of church and state. Well I knew he wasn't right and asked him why he thought this, and that I wanted to see it in writing, etc. I told him the plan was to meet after school and not even meet during the day like other school clubs were so we would not cause any problems. Even though we could meet during the day which I said was the equal access law for all school clubs. Because if my group had to meet off school grounds then the other school clubs should have to do the same. This made the situation worse for me and I got a three page letter from him saying how I was doing things illegally from one announcement. I remember no students showed up anyways for the meeting. I remember just saying to this person that we could work it out so it doesn't cause any problems, there were only a handful of kids that wanted to be involved and we would meet in a classroom after school. I asked him why he was so against it and what he was afraid of. This guy was now more upset and had the district administrator, who had already sided with him, meet with me. So I tried to explain to him and show him the equal access regulations, first amendment rights document, and the school board policies, which showed that the Christian club could certainly meet like the other school clubs could. Again this made matters worse and he didn't even look at them. From this point on they would not talk to me and began to try to turn others against me and the club. There were some other coaches and volunteers that supported the Christian club and the administration met with them and told them not to be part of it and that what I was doing was wrong. At this point we were not even meeting on school grounds. They told me I could not even be involved with the Christian club off school grounds, like on the weekends or after school hours. None of this was right at all. They were very hostile towards the group and towards me. I now was continually praying about the situation and also looking for some help. The friends I had in the school did not want any part of the Christian club now like they had before and they knew what was going on was not right, but they were afraid of causing any waves or even getting fired. The year went on and these two administrators knew they were in the wrong, and they gave me additional duties at school or took other things away, which was showing how they were abusing power. I found no help from anyone, except some distant friends. I knew it was in God's hands and I wasn't going to back down, I told them I would still meet with the group on Saturdays off school grounds. They were offending the students' first amendment rights and mine as well. Their reasoning was I couldn't meet off school grounds on the weekends because I was an agent of the government working for the school and this meant 24 hours a day. How ridiculous. I didn't get paid working 24 hours a day. Well every year there is a day called "See You At The Pole", it is an opportunity for anyone in the community to get together at a local flag pole at a school or courthouse and pray for our country, our leaders, the town, the school, the students, etc. And every year they had this held in front of this school, in the front lawn, which was a ways from the school and about a block from the street. I took one of my daughters with me who was in elementary school to go pray at the pole that morning before school, I think it was around 7:00 a.m. I pulled up and nobody was around the pole and it was almost 7:00. I saw other people and students sitting in their cars in the parking lot. They were afraid to go out there. God said get up and go. So I went out there and then others came out and we prayed, it went great! Later that day I was called in to meet with the administration. They were saying that I broke the law by being out there and that I had to apologize to the other people there and to the people that might have seen me while they drove by. I had to apologize for praying at 7 a.m. These two guys were watching to see who would show up, no other teachers did but some parents and students did. I said I was there as a parent and community member, but they said that didn't matter. I asked them how I was supposed to apologize to the people that drove by and saw me because I didn't know who might have driven by. They suggested I put something in the newspaper apologizing. I couldn't believe how stupid this was, but satan uses people that will not resist him, especially if you are trying to give God any kind of glory and praise. Things got worse for me at that school. They were now telling me that I should be fired and that I needed to start looking for another job. I had always received good evaluations and I was pretty popular with the students and teachers, I didn't do anything wrong. I didn't think I had to go somewhere else, but I knew how unethical these guys were and that they would keep coming after me. They kept saying I wasn't neutral towards religion, but I was neutral, I told them I can't stop being a Christian person. I was doing what they told me to do. They said I should go work at a Catholic school. I told them that they were not being neutral but hostile towards religion. That went over well. I was pretty young at the time, I didn't get any lawyer or meet with the school board. I left it in God's hands. As the year drug on, these two guys came to me and said they were going to eliminate my position and name it something else, but I could apply for the new position but I wasn't the person they were looking for because I wasn't qualified for the new position. Cowards, big time. While this year was going on I had contacted a popular Christian Defense Organization. These two administrators would never give me anything in writing, so they would not leave a paper trail, and they would only meet together with me. Several times I mentioned that they said this or that and they would deny it. So I didn't have a lot to go on. But I kept the faith and it was a long year, I was pretty much emotionally drained. I knew this whole thing wasn't right, and that I would have to find another job. The year was about over and I had been working with this Christian Legal Organization now for almost the entire year. Nothing could happen fast and it wasn't really supposed to. It all happened in God's timing. The Christian Legal Organization did get the Christian student group back into the school right after I had resigned and God opened a door to another school for me and my family. The whole time those administrators had thought they had won but they didn't. I wasn't there but it really didn't matter. The Christian club was once again established for the following year. That school had to let the club meet like other clubs with the equal access law or lose their federal funding. It also made one of the popular t.v. Christian programs at that time when the pastor was talking about the spiritual state of the union, he used this situation at this school and this student Christian group as one of the examples as to what is wrong with this country and with our public school system. I didn't even know it was televised until someone at the school said they saw it that weekend. God's timing.

The Coach

The coach called and said, "Come on down here," I need you on my team for this big game to play. I said "no problem coach, I'm on my way.

I asked this time, "who are we going to play, what's the game plan and at what level"? He said strap it on; it's going to be the devil.

And the plan is going to be to spread the good news and to help the lost. I agreed-no matter what the cost.

He said, you're carrying the ball, so they will be coming after you. But no need to worry, I'll show you what to do.

So I put on the uniform, the armor of God for protection and power. The enemy met me, but I refused to cower. It made me strong and I could do no wrong.

The game was tough, but I fixed my eyes on the goal. It was in the end zone, but I didn't see the pole.

It was the cross, the place of victory, where I had to see the One. But there was one last drive that had to be done.

Jesus made the call to run and our Christian Club was now the ball. He said right up the middle, take it right at them and go for the score. You'll get some blocking and a whole lot more.

It was the final big call; our Christian club represented it all. Although it was a good run, the enemy cheated, cheap shoted, and went after the ball.

I was getting tired and bruised, it was a good fight, it went into overtime but we still had to make things right. I got taken down in the red zone, came up short and hit the ground. The ball came out into His hands but they couldn't take Him down.

I looked up and I wasn't alone, the savior had it now heading for the end zone. You see they forgot about Him, the greatest of all time. Who made the path easy for us to climb.

Man I felt so good, Jesus always comes through. Especially when they didn't expect Him, but we always knew. We won this game, bigger than a dream, because we said yes to be on His team.

The game is over, we are all proud and standing tall and I hope you will be ready to hear from the coach, for the next big call.

Years later I had this poem in a folder, I hadn't shared it with anyone. We were having an assembly and it happened to be in the folder with a lot of patriotic writings and poems, and inspirational messages that students could pick out for the assembly. I gave the folder to the students and one student did choose the coach, I didn't even remember it being in there and he read it. It just brought back a lot of memories and it was kind of emotional at the time, nobody really knew the meaning behind it, just me and God.

Chapter 8 School Number Two

Well the coach did call again. It didn't take long and I was promoted to being a high school principal at a smaller school. This school was in serious need of a Christian leader. The school also had a discipline problem. It seemed like a good fit, and it was. The first thing I did was to have the Pledge of Allegiance recited every day. By doing this we would acknowledge God daily, with the phrase, "one nation under God", and show our support for our country. I also knew God would bless this school by this simple act. A school's best security system is having God in the school. We started another student Christian Club. We also started a program called Religious Release Time education, in which by law, students can go off campus up to one hour a week for religious instruction. We scheduled prayer gatherings at the pole for See You At The Pole, and for the National Day of Prayer. We had a pastor group praying for the school weekly that I was a part of. We would bring prayer requests to the meetings. One year there, we had this student led Christian mission organization come in during the summer to stay at the school. They had over 300 students that painted area houses for free. They had Christian bands and activities at night and it went over amazingly well. There was a lot of evangelizing that happened that week. Probably the biggest impact we did was when we had a very good friend of mine who did school assemblies, come to our school twice a year. He visited another 35-40 schools in the area giving his message on how to make America a better place and how to be a good citizen, make good decisions, etc. He did tell them about Jesus being his personal savior at the end of his speech. He can do this giving his first amendment rights. His presentation went over extremely well at all of these schools. The kids loved him and he went back to some of those schools the following years. We never heard one complaint and he had a positive impact on thousands of kids and teachers as well. I also would fill in as a backup speaker at the local Baptist Church when the pastor was gone. Things were going well, God knew what He was doing, and we had one victory after another. I figured if I was going to be a principal, I had to do it this way. God had called me to do this and I could not go the route of status quo. I had to do what we could do legally for God, and thus have Him in the school. On top of this I applied for a federal grant for the school for physical education equipment and we won one of them, for $305,000! I would publicly give God the credit for this because He had blessed the school. The Christian Club had grown to a good number of students, around 35 kids which was pretty good for as small as the school was. They were meeting during the day the same as the other clubs were. There were also a good number of kids attending the release time education program once a week. They would go to a church about a block away and some kids even gave their life to Jesus! Spiritually the students were never better off than they were at this time. We would have a yearly breakfast for the seniors and their parents. I would give a Christian and bible based speech to help motivate them for life after high school. I really felt good about that and they always seemed to like it and appreciate it. The other side to all of this was the number of attacks I was getting. Almost weekly there was a major problem, not with the Christian programs but personal attacks against me. With the major discipline issues, we had a lot of school board meetings in which serious decisions had to be made because the parents would appeal my decisions to the superintendent and board. The students here were not used to being suspended and being ineligible to participate in sports for serious behavior problems. By the way none of the students and parents that were causing problems participated in any of the Christian programs we had started. These students in constant trouble seriously affected the safety and well-being of the other students attending the school. We would have these parent and school board meetings which the parents wanted in order to get their kids off of suspension or to make them eligible again. These parents would attack my character and try to make the meetings about me and not about their son or daughter's behavior which caused the problem. The only thing I could do was stick to my decisions, pray and have others pray for me. These parents would also threaten with their lawyers and make false accusations against me. I would tell them that I did not even need a lawyer because what I had decided, I knew was right and would stand up in court, if it got that far. God gave me the strength and patience to get through all of that. He also helped me to be professional and to act like a Christian towards my enemies and I didn't try to get revenge or anything like that. I wasn't happy about it, but I knew God would handle it for me. I just had to be bold and stand firm, and not back down and defend myself as well. These meetings and this stuff was going on for several years now, but we were having great success with the programs we had started. God helped me to win at all of those meetings. Satan was trying to come after me because I was doing God's work; there is no doubt about it. That plan of his didn't work and the school hired a new district CEO. This time the enemy was going to attempt to get rid of and stop the release time program, the Christian Club meetings, the pole gatherings, and everything we had built up. This person was against these programs and I was now being questioned at school board meetings about what goes on at the club meetings and what goes on at the release time meetings. Even though that board had approved these things and they were invited to sit in on them whenever they wanted too. They now wanted to disband all programs Christian in nature. It was because of this new direction they wanted to go. There were not any complaints about what we had been doing from students or parents. The only change was that these programs had grown to include a lot of students and they were being very successful in helping students not only spiritually, but emotionally, and these students were doing better in school academically. The district administration and board could not now stop what they had already approved. Nothing was being done illegally and they had no basis to act on. The district administration started to take duties away from me and they said they would now take over some of my duties. Everything that you would expect or want in leadership, this school now did not have, despite my efforts. The schools decision to now have no Christian morals or values taught was what was coming top down from the district administration. Totally opposite to what we were doing and what we were role-modeling for the students and teachers there. It got to the point where other teachers were complaining about the direction of the school now and the district leaders and board. I tried to support the teachers and talk to the board about the teachers' fears and the way they were being treated, along with what was happening to me and the programs. I received zero support from that board and the board representative called me and said I should go be a pastor somewhere. The district administrator called me to his office and said he was elimination my position and that she was going to be the principal now. I told them I still had a contract for next year and they knew they were now in trouble. They were now denying they said this and again did not give me anything in writing. I prayed a lot about it. I had been there for five years now and I could have probably won with my lawyer, but God told me what to do otherwise. In the meantime the town of about 600 people had a petition going to keep me there with about 350 signatures supporting that. That sure made me feel good! I knew I had done God's work, I had always prayed for guidance to make the right decisions, and I always went home with a clear conscience. There was going to be a board meeting and supporters were there supporting me and saying the district administrator and board representative were making a mistake. I had done nothing wrong and had very good evaluations and support from the community and teachers. None of this made any sense. I did say as mentioned earlier, that I always tried to do what was in the best interest of the students and the school. I had loved my job there and we had accomplished many good things. I said I always prayed to God for guidance and He always showed me what to do, and that I was praying for everyone there at that meeting. God wanted me to demonstrate His love and how I should represent Jesus. I had talked a lot about that but I had to walk it now and not just talk it. I said to the people there that they need to keep these things going that we had started, that it was up to them now, even if I wasn't going to be here, we are all still winners. I left and felt great. I resigned the next day. God had other plans for me. He found another place for me to go which I later found out that a group of Christian community members had been praying for five years for a Christian principal to come to their school. There were a lot of needs here and I would do what God wanted me to do here now. I fought the good fight and I was going to finish the race. I had kept my faith, that's all that really mattered to me. I had to lose so I could win.

Chapter 9 Lessons Learned

The following are some important things that I learned from the experiences I had. Hopefully they will be beneficial to you as well.

1. Take The High Road: This means that you should always try to do what is right. It means to be the bigger person. It also means to give the other person the benefit of the doubt if you think they did something wrong to you and might of hurt your feelings. It really means to forgive and forget-it's hard but it can be done. You don't always have to respond back to someone or their accusations right away, give it to God.

2. Make Decisions and Stick With Them: I learned this lesson early on and it will help you to gain respect. Try to think it through first, but sometimes you don't have that luxury. People might not agree with what you decide but they will respect you for it. Always try to get as much information from others before you

make a decision if you can. When people feel pressure, then they tend to give in to changing their decision. Stick to it if you feel you made the right call. People don't like someone who is supposed to be a leader that is wishy-washy. Unless you were totally wrong or way-off stick with the decisions you make. Always pray and ask for guidance, God will help you even if you don't have a lot of time to decide, a quick prayer is always better than none.

3. See Through The Smoke: This means that things are not always as they first appear. Don't jump to conclusions when you have a situation to deal with. There are always two sides to a story and even more so, sometimes a right one. I have found that you don't have to bite on something or over-react because other people want you to. Wait until the smoke clears if needed and be patient.

4. Little Things mean the most: It seems we get few opportunities to do something big or earth shattering at our jobs or even at home. Sometimes those opportunities are there for those "big" things. Most of our time is spent on doing what we can and what is possible. If you put those two things together you will be doing the impossible. Also by going out of your way to do a favor for someone or by saying something nice to someone, even if you don't have too. These seem to be the things people notice and remember. Little acts of kindness will help to build relationships with people. With my daughters, we would have more fun doing activities in the back yard and just making

games up to play. To them it was just as fun or big as going on a trip or vacation. By giving your time and attention to activities that you can do plus if you do a lot of fun little things, they can add up to something huge. Give your time it's all we got.

5. Respond The Right Way: Always give an honest response or answer. Also always try to answer a question the best you can. People will appreciate this. If you don't know the answer, tell them you don't know, but you will try to find out and get back to them. It is best to be a straight shooter, but try to be tactful doing it. Some people have a hard time dealing with someone who is brutally honest.

6. Forgive and Forgive some more: Easier said than done, but it can certainly be done. Ask God to help you to forgive. He will send the Holy Spirit as a helper to help you do this. They say you can forgive but you can't forget, I don't really believe that. If you forgive, remembering it won't bother you anymore. Forgive and move on, life is too short. You don't have to tell that person you forgive them or what they did, just do it. Sometimes you have to clear the air with that person but then it is over and you might find you both have a better relationship or improved respect. But certainly don't try to get revenge or be passive aggressive towards that person. This will only make things worse plus it's not biblical.

7. Apologize If Needed: By doing this you can put a fire out. Calmly saying your sorry will be accepted by most people. It takes a big person

to do it, even if something wasn't totally your fault. You will get a new starting point to move forward. Nobody is perfect.

8. Don't let the past bug you: Past failures can help you or hurt you. Don't be a perfectionist. Everybody has made mistakes and have sinned; we all fall short of the glory of God. Satan will try to bring up past mistakes you have made, resist him. You can be a new person in Jesus Christ and Jesus has forgiven you. God will give you the confidence you need.

9. Qualities Needed: Having patience is an amazing strong quality to have. Most situations, problems, events, etc. require patience. If you have it and are willing to have more of it, then you will have an edge. It will give you power. God will make you wait, but He is never late. Preparation is another quality that is all about putting the time and effort in to whatever you need done. One great coach said the will to prepare is just as important as the will to win. Try to do your homework and keep your guard up. You don't want to get blindsided. Be non-judgmental towards people. If you are judging people then that will lead to sin. Try to take care of your own shortcomings. Everyone is different and they have their own set of problems or circumstances that they are dealing with. Have a caring heart. Helping others and living a life of service is the most rewarding kind of life to have. You have to ask yourself, do you want to make a difference or a living?

10. Have Fun And Be Yourself: The simple things in life are the best. Also reward yourself and

make time to do things that you look forward to doing. If all of your time is spent working than you are missing out. There is only one you and you cannot be replaced!

Chapter 10: Go For It!

God has a plan for you as well, as Jeremiah 29:11 says ,"For I know the plans I have for you declares the Lord, plans to prosper you and not to harm you, plans to give you hope and a future." (NIV). He has also given you spiritual gifts. Find out what they are, 1 Corinthians 12:4, says "There are different kinds of gifts, but the same spirit" (NIV). Why wait? God created us to love him, glorify him, and enjoy him forever. Get a new starting point and your life will be changed. It is never too late to start committing yourself to the Lord. Some people might be afraid or think they have to give something up. However, what you will get in return will be worth it. Some people think that God cannot or will not forgive what they have done in the past, but God forgives and the slate is wiped clean. The enemy is the one that reminds people of their past sins to produce guilt and anxiety. People need to realize that the enemy, Satan, can and will put negative thoughts in their heads.

That's where it comes from, yet the enemy wants you to blame yourself for those thoughts. When this happens, mention the name of Jesus, for there is nothing more powerful than his name! Life can certainly be challenging and difficult at times. I don't see how people can live without Jesus in their lives, but the fact is they do not. They might appear to be fine and without struggles, but they are not. They usually turn to other things, like drugs and alcohol, or suffer burnout. These people are never content and have no peace. They rely on other gods or earthly things to make them happy. Just check out the news and see how some with fame and money are all messed up. They have gained the whole world but are on the path to losing their soul. Mark 8:36 says, "What good is it for a man to gain the whole world, yet forfeit his soul"? (NIV). It is best to give thanks to God for everything you have *right now*. Tomorrow is not guaranteed to anybody.

There really is no reason that a person should not believe in God and in his son, Jesus, as our savior. He gave us Jesus, the Bible, creation, our conscious mind, and thousands of people who were converted to Christianity because of Jesus, during his ministry and after he rose from the dead. You will also know, for yourself when you commit yourself to Jesus, you will be a new person and things will never be the same. Look at science: they are discovering more evidence of biblical truth all the time. Noah's ark has been found, right where the Bible said it was, on Mount Ararat. They have found chariot wheels and shields in the middle of the Red Sea, where Moses crossed. Goliath's belongings such as his eating utensils and some of his armor were found. These items dated back to the time and place where he lived. They also had his name on them and were made for a person around nine feet tall. The Shroud of Turin, the burial cloth of Jesus has proved to be authentic. The list goes on.

Those who have Jesus in their lives are different. People can sense this as well. You don't have to be perfect—there was only one who was and he was put up on the cross. Some days it's two steps forward and one back, while some days it's one forward and two back. God will pick you up and brush you off and get you on track again. You might lose some rounds, but you can still win the fight.

If you have God with you, who can be against you? Everything belongs to him and he is in control. Look past the problem and you will see him through the smoke. There was a great line from one of the *Rocky* movies: "It's not how much you can give out. Its how much you can take and still keep moving forward." God will keep you up and moving forward, but you have to ask. In one of the *Terminator* movies, Schwarzenegger is damaged by the newer Terminator he is fighting and gets a steel rod though him, shutting him down. It's not over, though. He finds an alternate power source that gets him back up and functioning again. That's the kind of energy and power that God will give you when you think it's over. Philippians 4:13 says," I can do all things in Christ who gives me strength" (NIV).

I wasn't going to be at one school I was at much longer, due to the unethical behavior of the people in charge of the school, but it was God's plan. He does allow these things to happen. This helps you to realize that he has a better plan for you somewhere else. If a door closes, he will open another one. He knows when you have had enough. There were many people there to support me and our programs at this meeting. I told everyone that I loved working for the students, I loved my job, I prayed about everything for God's guidance, and I always had a clear conscience when I went home each day. I was proud of what we had accomplished and encouraged them to keep those things going for the students, even though I would not be there. We were all still winners. Sometimes we have to leave behind what we can, plant some seeds and move on. We don't always see the immediate results; sometimes they do not appear for a long time, sometimes not until we get to heaven.

Teddy Roosevelt said it best:

It is not the critic who counts: not the man who points out how the strong man stumbled, or where the doer of deeds could have done them better. The credit belongs to the man who is actually in the arena, whose face is marred by dust and sweat and blood: who strives valiantly: who errs and comes short again and again: who knows the great enthusiasms, the great devotions: who spends himself in a worthy cause: who, at the best, knows in the end the triumph of high achievement, and who at the worst, if he fails at least fails while daring greatly, so that his place shall never be with those timid souls who know neither victory nor defeat.

I often used to ask God, why did you pick R.T. as my dad? The answers I got: to make you the person you are today. Maybe he was the only one who had the right DNA to make me the way God wanted me to be? He was just the person I rode in on. I knew who my real father was and that has made all the difference in the world to me.

I asked for strength that I might achieve: He made me weak that I might obey. I asked for health that I might do greater things: I was given grace that I might do better things. I asked for riches that I might be happy: I was given poverty that I might be wise, I asked for power that I might have the praise of men: I was given weakness that I might feel the need of God. I asked for all things that I might enjoy life: I was given life that I might enjoy all things. I received nothing that I asked for; all that I hoped for, my prayer was answered.

—"My Prayer Was Answered," by Singspiration, from *Praise Our Songs and Hymns Supplemental Readings*, 1979.

It is easy to go to Jesus, but what he did for us on the cross was not easy.

If you with confess with your mouth, "Jesus is Lord," and believe in your heart that God raised him from the dead, you will be saved … for, "Everyone who calls on the name of the Lord will be saved." Romans 10:9–13 (NIV)

Suggested Prayer of Commitment

Lord Jesus, I need you. I realize I'm a sinner, and I can't save myself. I need your mercy. I believe that you died on the cross for my sins and rose from the dead. I repent of my sins and put my faith in you as Savior and Lord. Take control of my life, and help me to follow you in obedience. In Jesus' name. Amen.

The Dash

I read of a pastor who stood to speak at the funeral of a friend. He referred to the dates on her tombstone from beginning to end. He noted that first came the date of her birth and spoke of the second date with tears, but what mattered most of all was the dash between those years. For that dash represents all the time she spent alive on earth; and now only those who loved her know what that little dash was worth. For it matters not how much we own, the cars, the house, the cash. What matters is how we live and love and how we spend our dash. So think about this long and hard:

are there things you'd like to change? If we could just slow down enough to consider what's true and real. For we never know how much time is left to understand the way others feel. To be less quick to anger, and show appreciation more: and love the people in our lives, like we've never loved them before. If we treat each other with respect and more often wear a smile, remembering that this special dash might last only a little while. So, when your eulogy is being read with your life's actions to rehash. Would you be proud of the things they say, about how you spent your dash?

Linda Ellis

So that's it. It's up to you now, God Bless and good luck!